Navidating

EQUIPPING COUPLES TO NAVIGATE
THE MODERN DATING WORLD
WITH GODLY PRINCIPLES

[a 15-day devotional *for her*]

Edited and formatted by Katie Erickson

ISBN-13: 978-1973883241
ISBN-10: 1973883244

Friend,

I'm so glad that you've chosen to do this study! I'll tell you right from the start that it's going to challenge you, dare you not to overlook the little things, and equip you to build a solid, Godly relationship—just so you know what you signed up for.

Here's how it works: The first day is an individual study that you will work through on your own. Read through the devotional and respond to the study questions on your own. Think of this day as a personal heart check and challenge to get you started. Then, for days 2-15, read through the daily devotional and study verses on your own, then share what you learn and work through the discussion questions with your guy.

I hope that throughout, you'll keep your eyes fixed on Jesus and apply the truths shared in these pages to your individual life and your relationship. Everything I share is written with love and intentionality to help YOU build a meaningful relationship with both God and your guy.

I'm also committed to being really honest with you. I know I struggled with some of the same things you might be. I want to share what I learned through my time dating Matt, and to equip you with what works when it comes to dating in a way that honors God.

I hope that over the next few weeks you will grow closer to God and learn something new about how to have a healthy, Godly relationship. I pray that helps your relationship, and that it will make a difference in your personal faith as well.

~ Jordan Lee

Table of Contents

Day 1: Woman of God

Verses to Study: Proverbs 31:10-31, 1 Peter 3:3-4, Proverbs 19:23, Proverbs 22:4

The day after Matt and I met in college, I expected him to text me and ask if I wanted to hang out again sometime. But he *didn't* text me. In the middle of the afternoon, he called me to ask if he could pick me up at 7:00 for a date.

What? Seriously?

After getting over the shock of his intentionality, I agreed. At 7 o'clock sharp, he didn't text me to tell me he was there. He knocked on my door, walked me to his car, and opened the door for me.

I couldn't remember a single time that a guy I had just met worked up the courage to call me, ask me out, pick me up, and hold the door for me.

And I loved it!

However, it makes me sad that it was considered so rare and that now days it seems even more rare. While it's definitely a man's responsibility to step up to the plate, I believe we as women have a big part to play because so much of it is how we receive it and the message we send.

We live in a world that is beginning to program women to believe they can (or should) do it *all*.

While I'm the first to encourage a woman to be the beautiful and strong person God created her to be, we have to remember to look at beauty and strength through a Godly, eternal lens. Scripture gives us a glimpse into what a virtuous woman with unfading beauty looks like.

Grab your Bible, open it to Proverbs 31, and read through it.

Then, consider Proverbs 31:30, which describes a virtuous woman as a woman who fears the Lord, not as a prideful or overly independent woman.

A woman who fears the Lord is dependent on Him and trusts Him and His design. She's a woman of character and integrity, meaning she is honest and trustworthy. She is strong and a hard worker, not for the sake of proving herself but instead to honor the Lord and serve her husband. It's not for her own glory. This is where extreme ideals of the worldly view of women can get off track because they tend to make it all about power and glory for the self and not for God.

1 Peter 3:3-4 tells us that unfading beauty is not external but internal.

This is not saying that you should never do your hair or dress nicely but it *is* saying that your beauty and worth should not lie in those things. True beauty is not about what you can prove to the world on the outside through your accomplishments or accolades, but it's about your heart, in a humble and quiet spirit.

This doesn't mean that you can't have a voice or a successful career; it's about something deeper. It means that you revere Christ above yourself.

When a woman always tries to prove she is right and independent, she forgets how dependent she really is on the

Lord, and therefore she misplaces a humble, gentle, quiet spirit that honors the Lord. I know that for me personally, I often feel the deep desire to prove I'm right, and that can quickly lead to a downward spiral if I'm not careful. While strength is attractive, anger and pride are unattractive. God hates pride, and pride can take many forms!

Although many like to write these truths about beauty off as outdated, these are really the only ones that will stand the test of time, because they're part of God's design. They are intricately part of our soul and how we are made. We are the ones whose minds are constantly changing but God's standards and truths are everlasting.

Our world's standard of beauty and its idea of what makes a strong woman, on the other hand, is constantly changing. For example, a long time ago, being heavier was the ideal body type as it used to be a sign of wealth because it meant you were well-fed, whereas today being skinny or fit is often considered the world's standard.

Another example would be that in some parts of the world women are not just led by men but also oppressed. This is extreme and an abuse of power. That never part of God's design. Women are valued and adored daughters of God and should be treated as such.

However, almost the opposite extreme also exists in Western culture. It's as if there's a deep desire for a power shift, which is also not part of God's design. Sometimes, mainstream media almost excuses it as okay for women to dominate men now. How is this any better than men dominating women? Doesn't that hurt our society just as much?

The reality is that there are deep problems and repercussions when we operate in either extreme described above, because neither are in line with God's design. God's design says men and women are designed to complement one another, not compete with each other. A man is to lead in a Christ-like way, not domineering but like a servant. A woman is made to be his helper.

Yet many women scoff at verses like Genesis 2:18, which refers to the role of woman as being a "helper," because it sounds inferior or less important.

However, we need to understand what that means before we write it off so quickly. Tim Keller and his wife, Kathy, teach in their book *The Meaning of Marriage* that God describes Himself as a Helper (see John 14:26), and therefore it's an elevated role Biblically.

"The future is female" is a common phrase that modern women say to celebrate strong women. Most don't mean any harm by it, but if you look a little closer, it basically says, "We have no use for men."

Just think about that for a second. A human race cannot continue if this mentality were turn into a reality. Men and women need to work together for society to flourish.

From a young age, boys are being programmed by society to believe they don't need to be brave or masculine or have any sense of leadership. They are told they are disposable and no longer needed with phrases like these floating around. We need to be more careful about our word choice and how we value men.

Now, I'm not blaming women. Men have responsibility in this, too. It's no longer the women who are saying, "Chivalry is dead." It's the men who now believe it.

However, this devotional is about being a woman that honors God and respects His design—and that requires humility. Girls, you can be a strong, beautiful, and capable woman without totally emasculating a guy.

It's in a man's nature to hunt and gather, or in other words, to provide. Affirm him in kindness when he opens the door (or encourage him to if he doesn't), listen to and value his opinion, let him teach you things or pick up the tab, encourage him to be a servant to God and a servant leader to his peers, friends, and even you.

Be a woman of beauty, of a gentle spirit and a humble heart. Remember that men need to be respected and feel needed. Don't strip a guy of his manliness by being a "know it all" or being so proud and independent that you never come alongside to help or ask for help yourself.

As I said, this doesn't mean you don't have a say, that you should never have your voice heard, or that you can't be successful. It means to value your role as a woman and revere Christ.

So, part of being a woman of God and a woman who is truly strong and beautiful is to be a woman who fears the Lord, works not for herself but for God, and does so by honoring His design. Encourage your man, discipline your tongue, and guard and humble your heart.

This is not all about you and your independence. It's about God and your utmost dependence on Him, regardless of your romantic relationship status!

STUDY SECTION

Proverbs 31:30, which describes a virtuous woman as a woman who fears the Lord. A woman who fears the Lord is dependent on Him and trusts Him and His design. She's a woman of character and integrity, meaning she is honest and trustworthy. She is strong and a hard worker, not for the sake of proving herself but instead to honor the Lord. It's not for her own glory.

1 Peter 3:3-4 tells us that unfading beauty is not external but internal. This is not saying that you should never do your hair or dress nicely. It *is* saying that your beauty and worth should not lie in those things. True beauty is not about what you can prove to the world on the outside but it's about who you are—your character, humility, faith and gentleness.

REFLECTION QUESTIONS

What were God's original roles for man and woman? What does that look like in your life now?

What has been your stand—have you been following God's design or your own preferences? How do you set yourself apart as a woman of God?

How do you see yourself as being different because of God's design for you than what the world says you are?

How do you strive to help men step into the role God designed for them instead of discouraging them from it?

What have you done to encourage or appreciate a man when he has shown you respect and chivalry?

This is not all about you and your independence. It's about God and your utmost dependence on Him.

Day 2: Do You Live Up to Your Own List?

Verses to study: Mark 9:35, Proverbs 15:33, Matthew 7:3-5, James 4:4-8, Jeremiah 17:9

If you're like any other Christian girl, you probably have a list of criteria for your dream guy, or that you expect your boyfriend to live up to. I know that I did. My list included things like: he has to love Jesus, he has to be a man of character and honesty, he has to be someone I'd want my future son(s) to grow up and be like one day, he has to have a servant's heart, he has to respect me and my purity, he has to be hardworking, and it'd be nice if he had a nice smile, a solid family, and a good sense of humor.

Look at that list. All good things, right? Right. We should have standards. However, I think that when we obsess over a list of criteria for someone else—almost formulating a dream guy in our heads—we get so wrapped up in finding the right person that we can easily lose sight of the importance of becoming the right person.

Are you considering the Godly traits and characteristics you ought to be disciplined in as a woman? Or are you just posting all over the internet that women deserve great, Godly men—without considering what a great, Godly man also deserves?

Sometimes we have to do a heart check and remember to also grow in Godly discipline ourselves, to try new things, and to be well rounded so that we're not totally boring to talk to.

We need to learn to walk in our true identities so that we are strong, but not too proud, for a good, Godly man.

Focus on growing yourself in more ways than one, in spite of your relationship status or how well your guy is meeting certain criteria. Instead of obsessing over the perfect guy, pursue Christ your Perfecter and focus on being a better reflection of His love. Focus on depending on God and living up to the standard you set for others.

Your guy and your relationship will thank you for it.

STUDY SECTION

Jeremiah 17:9 tells us that our hearts are deceitful above all things. This means that we often believe we're doing better than we really are, which is why it's so important to humble ourselves and take a closer look at our hearts before looking at others.

Matthew 7:3-5 tells us that we often notice the speck, or imperfection, in someone else's eye instead of looking in the mirror and noticing the log, or imperfections, of our own. We tend to criticize others before holding ourselves accountable.

DISCUSSION QUESTIONS

Are YOU living up to the standards you set for someone else? Do you have a servant's heart, or do you serve yourself most of the time?

If you look in the mirror, how well are you reflecting Christ yourself? Instead of only focusing on what you want in a future spouse, also focus on who you are called to be for your future spouse. This season of dating is preparing you for that.

Girls: What do you want to bring into a dating relationship and eventually a marriage—baggage or beauty?

Ask your significant other: How well am I living up to Godly standards? In what ways can I improve?

Don't be so wrapped up in finding or having the right person that you lose sight of the importance of becoming the right person.

Day 3: Communicate Your Values + Beliefs

Verses to Study: 2 Corinthians 6:14, Proverbs 22:6, Joshua 24:15, Romans 12:9-21, Philippians 3:14

A friend of mine recently told me that in today's dating world, it's considered far too personal and forward to talk about anything too serious when you're first getting to know someone. As sad as that reality is, we need people to be brave enough to break through this cultural norm.

I mean, think about how ridiculous this logic is. Why would you wait until you've really fallen hard for someone, spent lots of time together, made memories together, and met one another's families to finally have an open conversation about your values? Why would you wait until your heart is really invested? Don't you think that seems a little backwards? What if you find out that you don't share common values on the big things?

I know that as a woman, it can be tempting to beat around the bush and try to guess what his values are instead of directly asking him. I know it's tempting to put it off because you don't want to scare away a guy that you really like. While that makes sense, please realize how important it is to discuss this kind of thing up front. It's not too serious or too clingy; it's wise.

Ideally your values on the non-negotiables like Scripture and family will line up, but if they don't, it's best to find that out sooner than later. Matt and I found our values lined up on the most important things like our shared belief in the Gospel, views on God's design for marriage, finances, political beliefs, and family values. There were certain specifics, such as traditions and preferences, that we had to be willing to compromise on in order to find common ground. We had to determine which differences we could work with and be flexible with to accommodate the other without compromising our personal values and convictions.

The reality is that two different people from two different families are bound to have differences.

If you don't take time to learn these things early on, it's going to be shocking when you find out that you have two completely different ideas of what's considered valuable, or when one of you feels as though you're dragging the other along.

These are important things to discuss while dating so that you understand what the other values early on. Of course, there will always be little surprises that pop up over time, but those should be things that you can negotiate on and work with.

Pray about how and when to have this conversation if you haven't already. Be sure that you find out if your values on the non-negotiables line up—that you are equally yoked— and you'll be better for it in the long run.

STUDY SECTION

2 Corinthians 6:14 warns us against being unequally yoked with unbelievers. What exactly does that mean?

Well, a yoke is a device that joins two oxen together and to the plow. If they are yoked unequally, that means one ox is stronger than the other and that makes it difficult for them to walk in a straight line and complete their task as a strong team. The stronger will likely be dragging the other along and bearing the burden of carrying the full weight of the plow. The two are at odds with one another and unable to work together toward a common goal, they'd actually end up going around in circles, never really getting anywhere.

This is why Paul warns against being unequally yoked—if one of you is dragging the other along instead of two people intentionally pursuing God and walking, it's going to be a huge burden for the believer.

This should be something discussed early on in your relationship.

DISCUSSION QUESTIONS

What are the things you can compromise on? What are your non-negotiables? Start with the little things and then discuss the big things.

Ask each other: what do you value most when it comes to relationships?

Do you want to raise and found your future family on God's Word?

Do you believe in God's design for marriage?

Have you accepted Christ as your Lord and Savior?

Do you have a personal relationship with Jesus? If not, what are your hesitations?

What core beliefs do we agree/disagree on? Is this something we can solve in a way that is Biblical?

How can we encourage one another in our walks with God so that we can press on toward Christ, both as individuals and in fellowship?

What are the non-negotiables for you? What are you willing to be more flexible on?

All dating relationships can end one of two ways: a break up or a marriage. It's never too soon to discuss the important things so you have a clearer idea which direction you are headed.

Day 4: Communicate Your Intentions

Verses to Study: 2 Corinthians 6:14, Ephesians 4:25, Psalm 19:14

I know that as a girl, having a boyfriend or a guy interested in you can feel like the greatest thing ever.

When I was in high school, my mom challenged me to look at dating through a more intentional perspective. She taught me that the reality is that dating ends one of two ways: a breakup or a marriage.

Even if you're not at a point in your relationship where you're ready to get hitched, you need to honestly consider what your intentions are long term. If you're just dating for the sake of dating and not even considering the possibility of marriage, you're dating without intention and instead just for the attention.

That's never healthy. I truly believe you shouldn't waste time dating someone if deep down you know that you don't see them as a potential spouse.

This isn't to be uptight but to protect both of your hearts. God tells us in His Word (see Proverbs 4:23) to guard our hearts above all else. If we're just letting ourselves fall in love with anyone, knowing full well we have no long-term goal, then we are not guarding our hearts. That's essentially living to satisfy our desire for companionship NOW without taking into consideration the other person's feelings or God's design for us.

Again, going on dates and getting to know someone is great, but should it turn into something more serious without any open, honest discussion about both of your intentions, it's wasted time and energy. Guard your heart by communicating your intentions, checking in, and moving slowly in the direction you both agree on.

STUDY SECTION

Ephesians 4:25 reminds us that God tells us to put away falsehood (aka, no hiding or beating around the bush) and that we are members of one another. In other words, as God's people, we have an obligation to be honest with one another. Communicating your intention is not just something that's nice to do but also something Godly. When you begin to see your significant other as a brother and/or sister in Christ, you're going to come to the understanding that being honest and upfront is not a favor but something you owe them as a fellow believer.

DISCUSSION QUESTIONS

What does dating mean to you?

What's your purpose for this relationship and for dating in general? Are you dating to get to know the person?

Have you talked about the important stuff, been friends for a while now, and ready to date to move toward marriage?

How can set yourself apart from the world and date in a way that is intentional, instead of just for attention?

Guarding your heart does not mean building walls. It means communicating your intentions, checking in, and moving slowly in the direction you both agree on.

Day 5: Communicate Your Expectations

Verses to Study: 2 Timothy 2:3-7, Colossians 3:23, Jeremiah 17:9, Philippians 3:14

I tend to have expectations as to how certain things will be. Sometimes, those expectations can be slightly unrealistic. Dating, especially now with all the pressure social media adds, can be one of many areas where we totally overthink and set expectations that aren't necessarily rooted in the Word.

When Matt and I were dating, I often expected every date to live up to every single one of my expectations. I'm not talking about the big stuff; of course, I expected him as a person to be honest, respectful, and Godly.

However, I also had some unrealistic expectations. I expected to get cute "good morning" texts from him and expected that I'd always be the first thing on his mind. I had this picture in my mind of the pictures we would take together, and all too often, those didn't quite turn out how I thought they would. In other words, I wanted every moment to feel like happily ever after because I wanted my relationship to feel as good as other relationships looked on the internet. This is because I had based my expectations on what I had perceived and what I had planned for the relationship, not what Matt and I had discussed or agreed on for our relationship.

So, you can imagine my frustration when a date would fall through or we'd end up arguing when the original plan was to enjoy a nice evening together. I wanted cuteness without having to curate intentionality. I didn't want to let go of my own ways, and obsessing over every detail consumed me.

Think about yourself. Have you ever fallen into a similar trap? Have you ever completely overthought something small, thus resulting in an unnecessary argument? Have you ever expected your guy to read your mind in one way or another? Have you ever found yourself wishing your guy did cuter things? Do you catch yourself wishing that he posted more photos of you on social media or showed you off to his friends more? Do you expect him to text or call you every morning and get frustrated when he forgets? Do you wish he bought you flowers just because, so that you could share on Instagram how cute your boyfriend is?

The list could go on forever but I'm sure you can answer "yes" to at least one of those. To be honest, these things in and of themselves are not bad desires.

However, I'm here to challenge *you* when it comes to these things. Because while these are all wonderful ways to be shown affection, the problem lies in how we prioritize these things and our motive behind wishing for these things. If we expect or desire these things simply because we want them, we're expecting the relationship to serve us rather than prioritizing our service to God within that relationship. We as women can tend to get wrapped up and totally overthink these extras – these details – instead of prioritizing and expecting the stuff that's rooted in God's Word like sacrifice, honesty, trust, respect, purity, and prayer.

Scripture reminds us that in EVERYTHING we do, including dating, we are called to ultimately work hard to serve God, not ourselves. Therefore, all of our efforts and expectations should be directly channeled to accomplish that purpose. When they are, we won't sweat the small stuff. The small details and unimportant things won't distract us from the real purpose so much. The victory we experience through trusting in God and honoring His boundaries when our flesh and human desires want to play outside the lines will be that much sweeter.

STUDY SECTION

2 Timothy 2:3-7 reminds us that in everything we do (including dating), we are called to ultimately work hard to serve God, not ourselves.

Philippians 3:14 is another verse that challenges us not to be distracted by silly things, but instead to fix our focus on Jesus and press on toward the prize. Therefore, all our efforts and expectations should be directly channeled to accomplish that purpose. When they are, we won't sweat the small stuff. We will be able to shed the unrealistic expectations we may have and focus on what matters most. The small details and unimportant things won't distract us from the real purpose when we keep Christ at the forefront of our minds.

DISCUSSION QUESTIONS

Can you identify any unrealistic expectations you may have for the other person or your relationship in general?

What expectations do you have for each other that are non-negotiable?

How can you work to focus on the non-negotiables more while also being flexible on the smaller stuff?

Ask each other: In what ways can I improve living up to Godly expectations? How can I be a man/woman of more integrity? What areas can I be more patient? Etc.

In EVERYTHING we do, including dating, we are called to serve God and His divine plan, not ourselves and our own desires.

Day 6: Communicate Your Feelings

Verses to Study: Proverbs 28:6, Ephesians 4:32, Matthew 12:37, Proverbs 25:11

In relationships, honest is huge. We live in a world that says it's fine to talk all the time, do all the things dating couples do, but never actually have an open conversation about how we feel or make any kind of commitment.

I think that kind of thinking can carry over into and poison even the most established relationships. Maybe you've moved past communicating your initial feelings. You've both agreed you like each other and are interested in dating. Perhaps you even have an exclusive relationship.

If so, consider how honestly you communicate your feelings, not necessarily your romantic feelings but all your feelings. Does it make you uncomfortable when he holds your hand in public? Do you wish he called more? Would it help you if he took more time to listen? How do you feel about the time you spend together—is it life-giving or does it drag you down or make you feel guilty?

Communicating feelings isn't about whining and complaining or sitting and ogling over each other with a million cute text messages and love letters. It's more than sending flowers or buying his favorite food, although doing kind things like these are good.

It's about being honest, transparent, and intentional within the day to day. Communicating feelings regularly, about the person but also about the state of the relationship and your own heart, helps establish a relationship based on honesty and communication.

If your guy doesn't do this, encourage him to. If you don't do this in a way that is mature and productive, I challenge you to consider how you can best communicate your feelings on the big issues, as well as build him up by reminding him how much you care about him.

This type of vulnerability and honesty is key if you wish to have a healthy, Godly relationship that is headed somewhere.

STUDY SECTION

Matthew 12:37 reminds us of the importance of how we use our words. Are we using them intentionally and to communicate in truth and honesty? We will be held accountable for the words we speak and how we speak them. It's important to remember this when it comes to sharing your feelings with one another, so that you do in a way that is productive, kind, intentional, honest, and loving.

DISCUSSION QUESTIONS

Do you communicate with Him? If so, how?

How can you reflect that in your communication with one another?

Have you communicated how you feel about one another?

Have you discussed how you feel about certain situations, behaviors, and issues? If so, have those discussions been face to face or just through texting? If not, what steps can you take to communicate your feelings in a mature way?
QUOTE PAGE

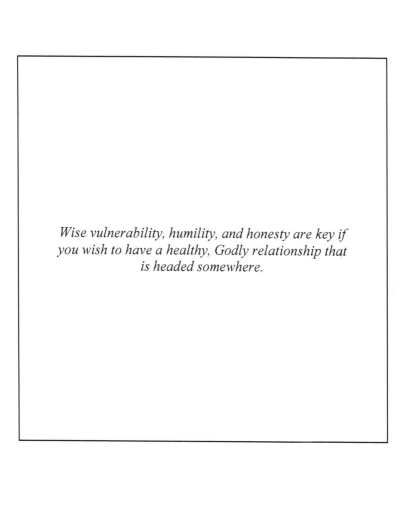

Wise vulnerability, humility, and honesty are key if you wish to have a healthy, Godly relationship that is headed somewhere.

Day 7: Communicate Your Boundaries

Verses to Study: Psalm 139:23-24, Ephesians 5:1-4, Mark 9:42-50, Galatians 6:2, James 5:12

A few weeks into our dating relationship, we had to have a pretty serious discussion. We talked about our physical boundaries and our expectations for the relationship. This wasn't to make the relationship too serious too fast, but instead to be sure that we were both clear on where we stood and how the dating relationship would operate.

Although we set boundaries and explained our expectations, there were times in our relationship where we would have to evaluate how well we were really sticking to them. Were we pushing the limit? Were we following through on what we decided? Had we met the other's expectations for things like communication?

Dating with Christ at the center requires having honest discussions and honoring your word, regardless of how 'serious' the relationship is yet. When feelings and romance get woven into two different people's busy schedules, it's even more important to be on the same page. That doesn't mean you have to get married tomorrow. That doesn't make you weird. It makes your relationship mature, intentional, and honorable.

Part of communicating requires communicating your boundaries. Setting some boundaries is wise if you are trying to create a healthy, God-honoring relationship. Boundaries can include agreeing on how much time you will spend together each week (don't make each other your whole world) and deciding how late you will hang out at night.

It also includes clearly establishing your physical boundaries. When it comes to this, it's really not enough to simply say something like, "I want to wait to have sex until marriage."

I mean, that's a good first step. But it leaves a lot of gray area, don't you think? That leaves questions like, "Does that mean you're open to doing everything else, or does that mean you don't feel right about doing anything until marriage?"

Boundaries should be set in such a way that it's not about barely crossing an imaginary line but instead honoring God in all ways.

If you're walking on a tightrope where one wrong step would drop you into the fire, you need to rethink your boundaries.

You need to ask your guy what makes it more difficult for him. Generally, women aren't triggered as quickly when it comes to physical intimacy. You need to understand that even if it doesn't seem like a big deal for you, it may be a big deal for the other person. It's important that you share what makes it most difficult for you to stop, and then also ask him to honestly share what makes it most difficult for him.

You may be surprised at what he says, but it's best to err on the side of caution and honor him as God's son and therefore, honor God—even if you'd totally love to snuggle on the couch. If he can't handle it and if it feels like you're teasing him, don't do it.

If you express an expectation or set a boundary together, honor that. Stick to your promises. Let your yes be yes and your no be no. Don't play games for attention or to make a point.

Honoring God isn't just praying together, not having sex, or putting Bible verses on the photos you post on Instagram together. Honoring God is also honoring your word and honoring one another. It's simple but often something we miss.

If you say you're going to call at 6, call at 6. If you've said no to certain physical behaviors, hold one another to that with honesty, love, and intentionality. If you've said you won't keep texting your ex, don't text your ex.

Let your yes be yes. Let your no be no. Don't play games when you're hormonal, emotional, or frustrated. Your heart (and his) will thank you for it, AND you'll be honoring God.

STUDY SECTION

Galatians 6:2 tells us to carry each other's burdens to fulfill
the law of Christ. Outside of just a dating relationship, we as
the church have a responsibility to each other, to help each
other carry the heavy burdens of this life and press on toward
Christ. By setting boundaries that are healthy, both physically
and with the amount of time you spend together, you help
one another carry the burden of temptation and the schemes
of the enemy.

DISCUSSION QUESTIONS

Have you thought about what your boundaries are?

Why are those boundaries important?

Are you initiating discussions about setting boundaries?

What boundaries need to be re-evaluated, or set for the first
time?

Would it be helpful to have accountability with this? If so,
who would be a good accountability partner for each of you
individually?

Let your yes be yes. Let your no be no. Don't play games when you're hormonal, emotional, or frustrated. Your heart (and his) will thank you for it, AND you'll be honor God.

Day 8: Protect Your Eyes

Verses to Study: Matthew 5:28, 2 Timothy 2:22, 1 Peter 2:11, Romans 10:13, Proverbs 4:23

A lot of people assume that it's just men who need to protect their eyes, but I believe it's women, too. Protecting our eyes is part of guarding our hearts and honoring God.

The truth is that women and men alike struggle with things like pornography. If that's you, I strongly suggest not letting that sit in the secret closet. Find a woman you can talk to about this and who can be your accountability partner. The more you talk about it and share it, the more accountability you have, and the easier it will be to find freedom. It's much easier to keep living in sin if it's hidden in the dark. Don't try to fight that battle alone.

The same goes for your guy. If this is something he struggles with, you don't need to freak out. As much as it may hurt to hear (trust me, I know!), it's nothing personal against you. Men don't see it as we see it. It's not your burden to carry, but before you shut the door on him, pray for him. Take your emotions out of it for a second and him be accountable to you—as you would for any other brother or sister in Christ. Then, urge him to take ownership and find another man to hold him accountable as well. You don't have to rescue him from it, but you also don't have to condemn him for it.

Secondly, a sneakier thing that we need to be careful about when it comes to protecting our eyes as women is the media we consume. The reality is that things like Pinterest and chick flicks can be just as addicting as pornography. They can twist our understanding of what true love is equally as much as pornography does.

While it's not bad to watch a romantic comedy now and then, we as women have to understand how much those kinds of things are like emotional porn. Just like porn warps a person's expectation for sex, chick flicks can warp our expectations for the emotional side of a relationship. Both types of things can be damaging to our hearts and twist our understanding of what love really is.

I know it's fun to create wedding Pinterest boards and watch rom coms with your friends. I'm not saying not to do that now and then. I am saying to protect your eyes and guard your heart by being mindful of how much you are looking at all that stuff. It can be sneaky with how it can warp your expectations for your guy and your relationship. Real relationships are not a movie or a moment captured in a pretty picture on social media. They are a series of imperfect and messy moments between two imperfect people serving a perfect God. Each relationship will look distinctly different, with the exception of sharing the common characteristic of honoring God's design.

I guess my point here is that this topic isn't only for the guys. I encourage you to be intentional about protecting your eyes from too much of the internet and Hollywood ideas of love—those are planned and staged. Don't compare your relationship against them. Don't expect a real relationship to look like that, or your guy to chase you halfway across the country when you storm away angry.

There's so much more to it, and part of guarding your heart is not building brick walls that never come down. Sometimes it's as simple as protecting your eyes and therefore your expectations.

STUDY SECTION

2 Timothy 2:22 is one of many verses that challenges us as sons and daughters of God to protect our eyes. This passage warns us to flee from youthful passions and instead pursue the things of the Lord. Shielding our eyes from things that arouse lustful behaviors and instead replacing what we see with good things is one way to abide by this verse.

Proverbs 4:23 tells us to guard our hearts. Some people assume that means don't share anything personal and build walls around your heart to avoid getting hurt. However, you have to look at the second half of this verse. It says to "guard your heart, for **everything you do flows from it.**" We are told to guard our hearts from wickedness and darkness, because if we don't, wickedness and darkness is what will flow from our hearts (and therefore, into our relationships). Guarding your heart means being mindful of what you see and surround yourself with, so you don't put lies and poison into your heart but instead godliness and light.

DISCUSSION QUESTIONS

In what ways have you failed to protect your eyes and guard your heart?

What do you need to confess?

How can you be more intentional about holding yourself accountable to guard your heart and protect your eyes?

How can you best encourage one another and hold one another accountable for this?

Real relationships are not a movie or a moment captured in a pretty picture on social media. They are a series of imperfect and messy moments between two imperfect people serving a perfect God.

Day 9: How Far Is Too Far?

Verses to Study: 1 Corinthians 6:19-20, 7:1-2, 1 Corinthians 13:4-8, James 1:14-15

When I was 15, I *really* wanted to drive on my own. Waiting 12 months to get my license felt like pure agony. As the days dragged on, there were many times I considered taking mom's car out for a spin when she wasn't paying attention. To be honest, the only thing that kept me from doing it was fear. The car wasn't mine to drive and I knew I wasn't prepared to drive on my own, and feared I would forget something and get in a wreck.

As much as I wanted to drive, as much as I desired to drive, I knew there would be consequences if I did so illegally. When I finally got my license a year later, I was prepared and legally able to drive. Finally taking my first spin around the block with a license in my hand made all the waiting so worth it. I had nothing to hide or fear.

I know the whole waiting until marriage concept is a heavily debated subject, especially when we're in a relationship. Contrary to popular belief, this design isn't set up to turn us into prudes but instead to prune us, prepare us, and protect us.

I think the feelings I had that year when I was 15 can relate to what waiting in dating is like. The Bible tells us that there are parameters for which to operate when it comes to sexual relations, just like there are parameters in which to operate when driving a car. If we operate outside those parameters, such as driving a car that doesn't belong to us or driving before we are licensed to do so, it can be destructive. The parameters are there to protect us, not to harm us. It's clear that God set up parameters to protect us when it comes to sex, too.

We may THINK we are going to marry someone, but until we actually take the step to give up a part of our freedom and commit legally, spiritually, personally, and financially, we really can't predict the future 100% accurately.

I know the temptation is strong, trust me. It can be so hard to know where to draw the line, can't it? We want to keep our guy around, and feeling close to someone we love is part of human nature.

But sometimes we tend to ask questions like, "Well, how far is *too* far?" and "What exactly *can* we do?" Unfortunately, the Bible isn't super clear about the specifics, which is why asking "How far is too far?" is tempting. But in all reality, it's not really a productive question.

Perhaps the better question to ask is, "Does this action feel like it's bringing me closer to God, or does it feel more like I'm creating a loop hole?" If your answer to that question leans toward the latter, a good rule of thumb is that it probably qualifies as "too far."

Maybe you've gone too far. If so, relax and remember that all things are redeemable. But don't relax so much that you let it carry on just because you think it's too late. Every day is a fresh start, and I want you to remember that unless you actually get married today, the man you're dating now is not your husband *today*. He may be in two months. He may be in a year. But if he's not your husband today, then you are not authorized to have sexual relations with him today.

Think of sexual relations with him like me stealing my mom's car when I was 15. It wasn't something I was authorized to operate yet. Your significant other isn't authorized to you. In other words, He is ultimately God's and until you're ready to not only give your body but also your last name, your time, your energy, your finances, your life, and your commitment to him as a spouse, then it's not the proper context to be intimate.

As your relationship grows closer, remember to shift your perspective so that above all else, you seek to honor your body as God's, your man as God's man, and God as the Lord of your life and your relationship.

When you're establishing some boundaries and growing in your relationship, you also have to remember that this is not about creating a set of rules for a relationship. We are not made to function like robots. While we want to honor God with our bodies, we also want to be careful not to become legalistic or self-righteous about this, either. Purity goes so much deeper than what we do physically; it begins in our hearts. God cares most about our hearts. A pure heart is one that sees herself and her significant other as God's precious creation, bought at a price, and therefore desires to bring Him glory *because* of that. An impure heart is one that seeks to bring herself glory by obsessing over how pure she appears to the outside world.

You see, this isn't just about what you have or haven't done. I'm sure you've felt guilty about something at some point and if not, you may down the road. In those cases, I urge you to confess it and discuss it. Trust me, when Matt and I were dating, we definitely had our fair share of uncomfortable discussions about this. We learned that if we are too general or not clear about our understanding, it can actually make it much harder. It's important to be on the same page and sometimes that means being detailed and specific. Transparency isn't always easy but it's the way to go.

Then, I urge you to drop it and press into God's heart, not into trying harder. What? Did I really say that? Yes. Why? Because while it's important to take action steps to honor God with our bodies, and to confess when we've done wrong. Dwelling on it and obsessing over it is actually dishonoring God because it almost turns the idea of purity into an idol itself.

Think of it this way: When I obsess over and try to create my own purity instead of pursuing the pure heart of God, that can be a slippery slope of self-righteousness, thus making it more about me and less about Him.

I found that it helped Matt and I during our dating relationship to have consistent, specific conversations about how we were doing.

We stopped asking, "How far is too far?" and instead started asking, "Does this bring us closer to God, or does it make us feel guilty?"

Asking "How far is too far?" basically sets you up for failure, because it's ultimately asking how close to the line you can get, which makes waiting ten times harder—especially in the heat of the moment.

When you're right at the line, crossing over it is way easier than if you're further from it.

So, if the answer to, "Does it honor God?" is NO, then it's wise not to do it. This will help you maintain a pure relationship and a pure heart.

So, my encouragement to you is to focus on God, first and foremost. Pursue purity, but also be mindful not to twist purity into the god you worship.

Make your actions more about honoring God and not just barely avoiding crossing a line. It's not a game and it's not about achieving some level of purity. It's about God and His beautiful design for you.

Worship God fervently and consistently, and the boundaries and waiting won't seem so suffocating. In fact, you may actually celebrate them because when we seek God, our desires will look more like His desires for us. His desire for us is better than what we think we want right now anyway.

STUDY SECTION

1 Corinthians 6:19-20 tells us that we are not our own because He bought us at a price. You belong to God and your significant other belongs to God. So, if that's true, we don't really have the freedom to do whatever we feel like or want to do with our bodies. We are to honor God with our bodies.

1 Corinthians 7:1-2 tells us that every man should have *one* wife. In other words, when we are joined together through sex and intimacy, that is a symbol of oneness that should be shared between man and wife. Even if you know that you will get married one day, if you have not actually stepped into that and committed yourself by taking marriage vows, you are not in a position to become one flesh.

DISCUSSION QUESTIONS

Have we already discussed our stand on sex and purity in our relationship? If yes, do we need to revisit that? If so, discuss it now.

What are the things that make you tick and that make it difficult to abide by the boundaries you have set? Be specific even if it's uncomfortable. Clarity is key.

Why does it honor God and how does it make our dating relationship stronger to operate within his boundaries and save sexual relations for the proper context of marriage?

Have we already crossed that line? If so, how can we take steps to ensuring we stand stronger next time? Would time apart be helpful?

Purity goes so much deeper than what we do physically; it begins in our hearts.

Day 10: Fellowship > Fairytale

Verses to Study: 1 Peter 1:13-16, Proverbs 27:17, Hebrews 10:24-25

"I just don't feel happy," I remember saying into the phone during our dating years. We had both experienced some big changes in our personal lives and it was weighing on our relationship and our ability to function in the same carefree bliss we had enjoyed when we first started dating.

He had graduated and was working toward a big dream, and I started to feel like a burden. As a woman, I wanted him to pursue me the same way he had the week we met. I wanted to feel that spark, the butterflies, the excitement and the *happiness* that we should feel when dating, right?

But things had gotten a little dull and I wasn't sure how to handle it. I remember his response to that phone call, "Well this can't just be about how happy we feel, J."

Woah. That hit me square between the eyes. He was so right.

The Western world has sold us on the idea that dating has to equal bliss. We've bought into the lie that if they fail to make us happy, we simply shouldn't date them. We believe that all the struggle needs to come after we say "I do" and that everything up until that point should be easy and carefree.

But there's nothing further from the truth and that's not God's design. Never once does God say in His Word, "I want you to be happy."

Disney and Nicolas Sparks sell us on a perceived reality of happiness that doesn't actually exist.

But God? God invites us into holiness, including our romantic relationships.

We are called to become holier, not happier. We need to make one another holier, not happier. We have to remember that happiness isn't sustainable 24/7. True, lasting joy comes as a result of walking in God's ways, in pursuing holiness, and living in His will.

Please understand: holy does not mean uptight or figured out. Holy means set apart and sacred. Relationships rooted in Christ are set apart from the relationships of the world. They aren't just based on personal fulfillment or feelings of happiness. While everyone is seeking feelings of happiness that won't last, set your focus on a holiness that lasts. Your relationship won't look like the world's, but it will reflect the Word.

So, the more we propel our significant other on toward God, the more we sharpen one another in the Word, the holier (and therefore, more joyful) we will be – even when the romance is iffy.

Don't expect your dude to make you happy all the time. He's a brother in Christ, not Prince Charming. First and foremost, you should each hold your own self accountable before expecting each other to hold you accountable. However, you two are first there to sharpen one another and spur each other on toward Christ. The reality is that flowers can only buy a limited supply of happiness. But the Father offers His endless holiness. Cover your relationship in THAT and you will find the fulfillment you're looking for in all those flowers and chocolates.

STUDY SECTION

Proverbs 27:17 tells us that fellowship is not just being together but sharpening one another, as iron sharpens iron. Helping one another become stronger followers of Christ above all else is a key component of a healthy and intentional relationship.

DISCUSSION QUESTIONS

Do you tend to look at your significant other as a romantic partner or a brother/sister in Christ first? Be honest!

What areas of your faith do you need the most sharpening and encouragement in?

How can you be a better encourager and friend before being a romantic interest?

Ask your significant other: How can I be helped or encouraged through my weaknesses (without being belittled) in both my relationship with Christ and as a person?

We are called to become holier, not happier. We need to make one another holier, not happier. We have to remember that happiness isn't sustainable 24/7. True, lasting joy comes as a result of walking in God's ways, pursuing holiness, and living in His will.

Day 11: Disagreements + Distance

Verses to Study: Colossians 3:12-15, Philippians 2:3-11

One year, we decided to drive to Florida with a big group of friends for spring break.

As we started the drive back to Indiana, Matt said, "Hey, we can stop at the Florida Georgia state line and take a photo!"

At the time, *Florida Georgia Line* was an up and coming band, so I loved the idea!

Shortly before we crossed into Georgia, I dozed off and took a little nap. When I woke up, I looked out the window and saw peach stands everywhere!

Did we pass the state line already? What about the photo?!

"Are we in Georgia?!" I asked.

"Yeah, you were sleeping and I didn't want to wake you up for a picture."

"SERIOUSLY?!" I exclaimed in disgust.

What can I say? I was disappointed (and a little tired). I pouted as I mumbled under my breath, which of course upset him, as he thought he had made the right call by letting me sleep.

Without warning, he angrily whipped the car around and started heading south, "Fine. You want your picture? You'll get it."

Ten minutes later, he pulled off the side of the road and made me get out and stand by the sign—alone—as he snapped the photo from inside the car. The photo was dark and the bug guts on the windshield made it hard to see anything. It was all pretty pathetic. Needless to say, we both had pretty sour attitudes at that point.

Our first argument as a dating couple was seriously pathetic. We fought over a stinking photo that turned out so horribly I don't even think we even saved it. It wasn't even worth the energy we wasted arguing about it in the first place.

We eventually had to talk about it. Although I was probably the only one in the wrong, Matt never treated me that way. He never tried to pass blame. He simply forgave me and took time to identify what he could have done better.

Then, he also apologized and asked me to forgive him for getting so angry and unnecessarily whipping the car around. That argument (as silly as it was) and how we solved it set the tone for the future arguments that would inevitably come.

Conflict is to be expected between two imperfect people. Just like we had a long distance to travel from Florida to Indiana, sometimes distance can occur between two people when they are faced with disagreements.

If you date long enough, or if you're faced with circumstances that make it difficult to communicate well, such as long distance, you're bound to butt heads at some point. Butting heads isn't really the problem, but how you resolve issues can become a problem.

Sometimes it's tempting to prove that we're right, and it can be very difficult to give grace when it is undeserved as well as to intentionally look at the specific ways we may be at fault, too. That's where humility comes in.

If you and your guy argue often, or if you have an on-again-off-again relationship, remember the call we have to treat others, even those closest to us, with compassion, kindness, gentleness, patience, and humility.

Harmony between two individuals, dating or not, is impossible if both people do not consciously try to choose actions that line up with the Word and operate out of God's truth.

The next time he upsets you, I dare you to be quicker to forgive him. Forgive when it makes no sense. Give grace when it's undeserved. Die to your pride, because Christ died for you.

STUDY SECTION

Colossians 3:12-15 reminds us to bear with one another and forgive one another as God has forgiven us. When we handle conflict, disagreements, and difficult circumstances with love (which means to be selfless and sacrificial), it is much more bearable.

DISCUSSION QUESTIONS

Is your relationship filled with more compassion or heated passion?

Do you approach conflict with a prideful or humble heart?

How have you been unkind toward the other?

Ask each other: What is one thing that you could improve to treat him/her more like a child of God?

> *Harmony between two individuals, dating or not, is impossible if both people do not consciously try to choose actions that line up with the Word and operate out of God's Truth.*

Day 12: Serving One Another

Verses to Study: John 15:13; Galatians 5:13; Romans 12:1,9-13; Mark 10:45, Matthew 25:40

When we first started seeing each other, I came down with a nasty flu bug. We weren't in a long term or serious relationship yet, but Matt still did what He could to help me. He took it upon himself to bear my burden, my sickness, and help me recover in every little way he could.

I'll never forget the day he brought over a big bottle of orange juice. My roommates snickered at the cuteness and my washed-out cheeks blushed in embarrassment but also in appreciation.

A few months later, he ran an errand for me when I was overwhelmed with work and school. He didn't do it because I asked, but because he knew I was stressed and he wanted to lighten the burden for me any way he could. Again, I was humbled and deeply appreciative.

Helping the person you're dating is so much more than just cute; it's Biblical, and it extends beyond romantic relationships. I think sometimes we forget that a boyfriend is a brother in Christ first and foremost.

Sure, we have a personal and romantic connection, but ultimately we have a deeper connection in who we are in Christ. If you are currently dating or considering dating someone who doesn't know Jesus, I urge you to reconsider, as the pain of being unequally yoked is not worth it later on.

That doesn't mean the guy can't ever make mistakes or struggle in his faith. It means he needs to at least be a follower of Christ and active in his faith. It's necessary for a long term, harmonious relationship—especially because relationships either end in breaking up or in marriage. Just consider that.

Anyway, here's my point: the guy you are seeing, whether you've been with him two weeks or two years, is one of God's creations. He's a man that God loves and a man you can help because that's what we are called to in Christ-like friendship, not just dating.

Sometimes I have a hard time asking for and accepting help from others. Maybe you're the same way, maybe not. Either way, don't forget the importance of bearing one another's burdens. Regardless of the type of relationship, it is Biblical for the church to bear one another's burdens as Christ bore our sins on His back. We act in Christ-like character when we extend a hand to lighten the load for another.

Remember, you are brothers and sisters in Christ before anything else, even when you're Facebook official. Look at your relationship as such and it will be fuller and more beautiful for it.

STUDY SECTION

Galatians 5:13 dares us to use the freedom we have in Christ to serve one another humbly in life. It's not about serving our flesh or our own desires, but honoring and loving the other as Christ loves us.

DISCUSSION QUESTIONS

Are you willing to bear each other's burdens?

What burdens can you help one another carry without overstepping personal boundaries?

How can you help one another resist temptation and work together toward a common goal of Christ?

How have you been willing to ask for help and allow someone to help you?

Do you see the need and do something about it just when it's convenient or at all times?

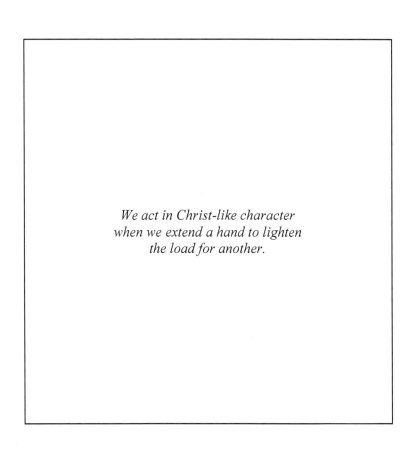

*We act in Christ-like character
when we extend a hand to lighten
the load for another.*

Day 13: Seek to Understand

Verses to Study: Matthew 5:27, Colossians 3:8, Ephesians 4:28, Psalm 19:14, James 1:19, John 13:15-17

One time I thought we made plans to go to ice cream after Matt got out of football practice. I called him and said, "It'd be fun to grab ice cream after you're done with practice!" and he responded, "Yeah, it would!"

You may be able to imagine my confusion when he never showed up or followed through on the date. After several hours of not hearing from him, I called him—fuming, I might add.

He didn't understand why I was so upset (which upset me even more, go figure). Turns out, he didn't realize we had actually made plans. To me, I thought we had both agreed to the idea. In his mind, we had just talked about a fun idea. We hadn't set a time or clearly said, "Yes, we are doing that. I'll meet you at ___."

It quickly became clear to both of us that our communication styles were very different. He had gotten used to being given a schedule and having coaches clearly tell him where to be and when. I wasn't used to that structure. I generally made plans by suggesting an idea and then if both agreed to it, we would just make it happen by texting a meeting spot around the time we would be ready to go.

Many will tell you that communication is key to a successful relationship, and that's true.

But I want to add a word to that: EFFECTIVE communication is key to a successful relationship.

Communicating is important, but taking the time to learn the other's communication style is even more important. Even if you live in the same culture and speak the same language, you will likely find that you still communicate and understand certain things differently.

This is usually due to many reasons, such as how you were each raised, the line of work you are in, the way your friend groups operate, etc.

Communication isn't just saying what you want but asking more questions and listening more intently to the heartbeat of another. It's getting to know the hard stuff and listening for the things we could easily tune out.

James 1:19 reminds us to be quick to hear. In other words, listen and pay attention to the way your significant other communicates plans, intentions, desires, interests, etc. Be eager and willing to learn his ways and understand him. Then, the passage tells us to be slow to speak.

When Matt didn't show up to take me out to ice cream, I was not slow to speak nor was I quick to listen. I was quick to call him and give him a piece of my mind, instead of first listening to his side of the story.

Regardless of how long you've been dating, you're getting to know each other and learning about each other. I don't think that ever really ends, even in marriage, because two people are constantly growing as individuals and together.

That being said, remember to give guy grace. That doesn't mean let him blow you off or treat you like an option. It means to hear him out before 'giving him a piece of your mind.'

Maybe he really didn't hear you or understand what you meant. Maybe he interpreted your feelings differently than you intended to express them.

I know that it's tempting to want to be 'right' when things don't go our way. When things don't go your way, I challenge you to do what I didn't do in that situation (but have slowly learned to do more!), and be quick to do what God says: be quick to listen for God's voice and to your guy, slow to speak, and even slower to anger.

While there is such thing as righteous anger, grace wins every time.

STUDY SECTION

James 1:19 tell us to be slow to speak and quick to listen. It's better for us to take time to understand instead of just assuming we know what someone means. When it comes to dating, be quick to listen to the other and learn about their ways instead of just assuming you know.

DISCUSSION QUESTIONS

Do you listen to understand or listen to fix? How can you listen to your guy better?

Is your priority to be right or to be fair?

Do you take words spoken to you literally at face value, or do you try to interpret if they may be meant differently? What steps can you take to be more effective at communicating?

Do you consider how the words you are about to speak will affect people they are spoken to, or do you just speak?

While there is such a thing as righteous anger, grace wins every time.

Day 14: Your Relationship as a Light

Verses to Study: Ephesians 5:1-2, James 4:4, Matthew 5:14, Luke 11:33

Some friends and I were watching a movie recently. The room was almost completely dark, the moonlight casting a shadow through the blinds.

Then, someone walked in and hit the light switch. Although the movie didn't stop, someone spoke up, "Hey! Turn the lights back off!"

The criminal who bumped into the switch apologized and hurried to flip them off.

Everything resumed to how it was the moment the lights dimmed again.

I tell you this story because it's kind of like an example of what is described in this passage. Acts 3:19-21 tells us that THE light has come into the world but humans hated the light because they loved the darkness.

Think about it. Just look at the modern dating culture (if you can even call it dating). The culture dares us to conform. It's normal, even encouraged, to shack up with a random cute guy from the bar on Saturday night. It's often considered more serious for two people to hold hands in public than to sleep together after a party on college campuses. It seems like *everyone* is active on dating apps. The broken dating culture we live in isn't just confined to college campuses, though. It's definitely more noticeable in places with tons of young people, but the brokenness exists both off and on university grounds.

Maybe you've experienced a guy totally disrespecting a girl. Maybe you've seen a girl totally disrespecting herself or living a double life. Maybe you've been that girl.

God isn't surprised by this culture. He isn't surprised by the godlessness that seeps into our culture. His Word was written ages ago yet still predicts this happening. He knew long before we ever did that our culture would be like this, and He warns us against it through passages like 2 Timothy 3:1-7.

Avoiding the brokenness of the culture can feel almost impossible when we are surrounded by it. Worldliness doesn't want its feathers ruffled. It's easier and expected that you just go with it. If you say anything that stands in disagreement to the loose-ness of it—if you shed any light on the brokenness of it—you're immediately called out like the person who flipped on the light switch and disrupted our movie night. The light disrupts what's going on in the dark.

Dating God's way in a world like ours is hard. Scratch that, living God's way in a world like ours is hard. Going against the grain and standing firm in God's ways can be really, really hard. But it's not impossible.

When Matt and I started dating in college, I was in a sorority and he was a starter on the football team. We were constantly slammed with messages about how to date in college. Everything around us said it was no big deal to sleep together, or to black out drunk together, and in some cases, even to cheat on one another if we felt like it. I mean, of course no one said this to us. But the world we lived in essentially said it was no big deal, that it was normal.

We were the weirdos who chose to be the nonconformists. That doesn't mean we never struggled or stumbled. There was a time we had to reset our physical boundaries and make them stricter because we had gotten lax about them. There were times we said things we regretted when we were upset.

In those situations, we had to have really honest and uncomfortable conversations to help hold the other accountable, but we also had to decide how we really want to live. Each time, we came out refined and stronger in our choice to serve God with our individual choices and with our relationship.

Try to shift your perspective from looking at your boyfriend as a partner in crime (although I know that's cute and stuff) and begin to see him as a *partner in Christ*. Companionship can be a gift and an opportunity to champion Christ in a culture that does not. That doesn't mean be perfect. It means be intentional, spur one another on instead of dragging the other down, and find ways to help the other shine God's light.

It won't always be popular, but your relationship can be a beacon of light in the dating world because part of Godly dating is fellowship.

Fellowship is holding the other up, spurring one another on toward Christ, and standing on solid ground in a world full of quicksand.

At times, your foot may slip into the quicksand a bit and you may feel as though you're sinking. You may experience a failure here or there. You may feel that the world around you is too strong and pulling you under. In reality, it's just your toes that got stuck in the sand and caused you to stumble.

The truth is that all of us feel more comfortable in the dark, but we aren't made to live there and there's hope when we slip.

The light of Jesus is the only hope we have, and living in the light can be uncomfortable but it's also critical. With a little help from each other and the Lord, you *can* pull your toes out, reset, and reclaim your ground.

When you live by the light, bring your own sins to the light, and keep walking in His ways, there will not a single thing in your life and in your relationship worth hiding.

So, be a light by reflecting God's Light. Be courageous and different in a world that's not. Go on real dates. Be selfless. Pray together and for each other. Encourage one another. Help each other up when you fall, hold yourself and the other accountable, bend down to serve the world around you, and stand firm when it's unpopular.

I promise, it's worth it.

STUDY SECTION

James 4:4 challenges us to remember that friendship with the world is enmity with God. You cannot live for or serve both—in either your personal life or your relationship. Your relationship will either bear witness to the Light by standing out from the ways of the world, or it will blend in with the ways of the world. Choose wisely.

Matthew 5:14 tells us that we *are* the light of the world and a city on a hill. If your relationship is rooted in Christ, it will inevitably stand out in the world and shine a light. Those living in darkness may not like it, but that's no reason to hide it or dim it. Light illuminates the darkness. Shine on.

DISCUSSION QUESTIONS

How am I reflecting Christ in our relationship?

Do I act the same to my significant other in public and in private?

How can we stand strong against the pressures of the world and have a godly relationship?

Ask each other: How can I better show you the love of Christ?

Be a light by reflecting God's Light.
Be courageous and different in a world
that's not. Go on real dates. Be selfless.
Pray together and for each other.
Encourage one another. Help each
other up when you fall, hold yourself
and the other accountable, bend down
to serve the world around you, and
stand firm when it's unpopular.

Day 15: Priorities

Verses to Study: Matthew 6:33, Matthew 22:37, Exodus 20:1-3, 1 Corinthians 11:3

Now that you've worked through this study, I want to say something important. Now, you either really want a Godly relationship, or if you've got one, you may catch yourself comparing it to someone else's. Maybe you feel like you don't measure up or meet the qualifications for a Godly relationship. Or maybe you've read through so many of these studies and thought, "Oh, good, we've already talked about that. We're way ahead of the curve."

But the reality is that we're never in as much despair as we think we are, but we're also never as good as we think we are. If we beat ourselves up for every mistake we've made, we essentially aren't trusting God's promises or believing who He says He is. On the other hand, if we think we're pretty figured out, we essentially make ourselves out to be as good as God when the Word tells us the exact opposite. We've all fallen short of God's glory and even our very best is never going to be good enough on our own when compared to God's standard. Both of these reasons reveal how desperately we need Jesus and the *gift* of grace.

So, to close this devotional I want to challenge you as a woman, regardless of how your relationship is going, to do a heart check and consider what you're prioritizing.

The reality is that right when we think everything is just the way we want it in our relationships, setbacks or unexpected problems may pop up. You may get hurt and you may even break up. When it comes to having a Godly relationship, sometimes we make one or two mistakes that can make the setbacks and conflicts that arise feel much bigger than they really are. They can damage our view of God if we're not careful.

So, my first challenge to you when founding a relationship on God is to remember to have your own faith. Cultivate your own relationship with God outside of the relationship with your guy. As you learned in this study, it's important to learn to communicate and be intentional about growing in fellowship and pushing one another closer to Jesus. However, it's equally as important (if not more) to be intentional about keeping your own relationship with God first and foremost. That way, your spiritual life won't be driven or dictated by the state of your dating relationship. If these relationships are *too* intertwined, it can cause your whole spiritual life and walk with God to plummet the second the relationship with your guy gets a little rocky or ends. The two relationships need to be independent of each other to prevent your own growth from being stunted or shattered if the relationship doesn't work out or faces difficulty.

Secondly, I challenge you to consider what your god is— what or who sits on the throne of your heart. If you're so focused on your dating relationship, the idea of a Godly relationship can quickly become a mini god in your life and that will also stunt your growth in your own walk with God.

I know from personal experience that it's easy to forget that a Godly or Christ-centered relationship does not equal a perfect relationship. There are going to be gaps and ways you both fall short. This can be a struggle for men and women alike, but women tend to spend more time journaling about their future husbands, crafting pretty future wedding Pinterest boards, and honestly just dreaming about the perfect guy instead of desiring our Perfect God. Be intentional about creating a Godly relationship, but don't idolize it. Your first concern needs to be building a relationship WITH God.

Why? Because your heart is a flower, and flowers only flourish when they're watered with the Word and planted in rich soil of Truth.

Lara Casey, an author and friend of mine says this, "Flowers grow through dirt." (*Cultivate* by Lara Casey, 2017)

I love it because it's so true! Mistakes, setbacks, and challenges happen in all aspects of life, including relationships, but they exist to teach us perseverance and how to grow through the hard stuff. They exist to help us rely on God as our God and not our guy as a false god.

So, if you want to flourish, build your personal relationship with God more than you build just your Godly relationship. You won't be settling, you won't ever be left lonely, and you won't be let down.

Remember this: prioritizing does not mean to be perfect. Prioritizing means to persevere in putting God before all things and to keep going when the work gets long, when mistakes are made, and when all you've got left is faith that God will get you through.

Keep God on the throne of your heart and you will flourish through all rain, dirt, and sunshine that both dating and life throw your way.

STUDY SECTION

Matthew 6:33 urges us to seek *first* His kingdom and His righteousness. This is one of many places in Scripture that challenges us to fix our focus on God above all else. God needs to be your first priority, and all other things will fall into place.

Personal heart check (reflect on this on your own): Does your relationship with Christ *really* come before the person you are dating? What is on the throne of your heart? It's tempting to just say that God is because we all know that's the right answer, but look a little closer. Follow the path of where you spend the most time, energy, and money to find out what you're really prioritizing.

DISCUSSION QUESTIONS

Does your relationship worship God, or do you worship your relationship as a god?

What intentional steps are you taking to encourage one another in your individual relationships with Christ?

How can you persevere in putting God first when the temptation to put your own desires first tries to take over?

Always prioritize a relationship WITH God more than just having a Godly relationship.

Closing Letter from Us

Hey!

You made it!

What did you think of the last 15 days? What did you learn? Were you challenged?

We hope that above all else, you were challenged to humble yourself, put God first, communicate about the important things, and work through the hard things.

We know that it can be hard to come up with date ideas that are creative, fun, and active. It's so easy to just sit around and watch movies together. While that's not a bad idea now and then, it can get kind of repetitive as well as create a space of temptation if you're always alone late at night, snuggling on the couch and watching movies.

So, to end this devotional, we wanted to give you a list of some of our favorite date ideas. Many of these were dates we enjoyed while we were dating (and still do even now that we're married!) and we hope that you have some fun and try some of them out, too!

In His Love,

Matt and Jordan

35 Great Date Ideas

1. Try a new recipe from scratch, make a fort, and pretend you're in a restaurant.
2. Make homemade popcorn and try lots of different seasonings on it.
3. Find a hole in the wall restaurant in your town and order the most exotic thing on the menu.
4. Play catch or frisbee at the park.
5. Google a town you've not been to within a couple hours, go there, have lunch, then turn around and come home. Don't forget to karaoke the whole ride!
6. Go fishing.
7. Volunteer at your local food pantry.
8. Try a cooking class, then eat all of it!
9. Pack up a basket and have a picnic.
10. Put on a nice dress and your dancing shoes. Go country line dancing at a local dance bar.
11. Find a quaint breakfast place and have brunch together.
12. Double date to a drive-in movie.
13. Go to a concert and take snap videos of you two rocking out (no shame!), or go to a sporting event and make fake bets on the game with popcorn or peanuts. Loser buys dinner!
14. Go hiking, but wear the silliest outfits each of you can find!
15. Have a campfire.
16. Build something together. One year we found some old pallet wood, dug up some nails and sandpaper and made a really neat coffee table. It'll go in our first house together!
17. Paint together.
18. Go to the shooting range.

19. Find an old-fashioned diner near you, throw some tunes on the radio, and order the weirdest thing on the menu.
20. Go to Walmart, pick up some water balloons, fill them up, and then have a water balloon fight.
21. Go putt putting or hit some golf balls at the driving range. Make it a competition. Furthest ball wins. Loser buys milkshakes.
22. Call up some friends, make some coffee and cookies, and play Apples to Apples.
23. Go for a tractor ride or four wheel around an open field.
24. Try a different cuisine. Our favorite was Thai!
25. Go to a carnival and ride the biggest ride (we recently did this and Matt almost lost his lunch but it was worth it).
26. Go watch a play or get tickets to a local sporting event.
27. Tune out technology all evening. Leave your phones and go out to dinner.
28. Go bowling or roller skating.
29. Check out a museum or aquarium.
30. Go for a long hike.
31. Sign up for a workout class or dance classes together.
32. Try tandem biking.
33. Race go-carts together.
34. Spend time with each other's families.
35. Go to an arcade and play a game. Loser buys dinner!

Made in the USA
Lexington, KY
27 February 2018